Seven Last Words

Seven Last Words

Cross and Creation

†

ANDREW McGOWAN

Illustrations by Bettina Clowney

CASCADE *Books* • Eugene, Oregon

SEVEN LAST WORDS
Cross and Creation

Copyright © 2021 Andrew McGowan. All rights reserved. Except for brief quotations in critical publications or reviews, no part of this book may be reproduced in any manner without prior written permission from the publisher. Write: Permissions, Wipf and Stock Publishers, 199 W. 8th Ave., Suite 3, Eugene, OR 97401.

Cascade Books
An Imprint of Wipf and Stock Publishers
199 W. 8th Ave., Suite 3
Eugene, OR 97401

www.wipfandstock.com

PAPERBACK ISBN: 978-1-7252-9826-2
HARDCOVER ISBN: 978-1-7252-9825-5
EBOOK ISBN: 978-1-7252-9827-9

Cataloguing-in-Publication data:

Names: McGowan, Andrew, author. | Bettina Clowney, illustrator.

Title: Seven last words : cross and creation / Andrew McGowan.

Description: Eugene, OR: Cascade Books, 2021 | Includes bibliographical references.

Identifiers: ISBN 978-1-7252-9826-2 (paperback) | ISBN 978-1-7252-9825-5 (hardcover) | ISBN 978-1-7252-9827-9 (ebook)

Subjects: LCSH: Jesus Christ—Seven last words—Meditations.

Classification: BT457 .M40 2021 (paperback) | BT457 (ebook)

03/12/21

Contents

I
CREATION and CROSS | 1

ONE
Then Jesus said, "Father, forgive them; for they do not know what they are doing." | 5

TWO
He replied, "Truly I tell you, today you will be with me in Paradise." | 9

THREE
When Jesus saw his mother and the disciple whom he loved standing beside her, he said to his mother, "Woman, here is your son." Then he said to the disciple, "Here is your mother." And from that hour the disciple took her into his own home. | 15

FOUR
"My God, my God, why have you forsaken me?" | 21

FIVE
After this, when Jesus knew that all was now finished, he said (in order to fulfill the scripture), "I am thirsty." | 27

SIX
When Jesus had received the wine, he said, "It is finished." | 33

SEVEN

Then Jesus, crying with a loud voice, said, "Father, into your hands I commend my spirit." Having said this, he breathed his last. | 39

II
CONVERSATIONS at the CROSS | 43

ONE
Judas | 47

TWO
Dismas | 53

THREE
Mary | 59

FOUR
The Father | 65

FIVE
Longinus | 71

SIX
The Silence of the Angels | 77

SEVEN
Nicodemus | 83

The first set of these sermons was given on Good Friday in 2016 at St Thomas Church, Fifth Avenue, New York City, and then in a different form at the University Church of St Mary the Virgin, Oxford, on Good Friday 2018. I am grateful to the Rev'd Canon Carl Turner for the initial invitation and to the Rev'd Dr Will Lamb for the second.

The second set was written during the later part of a sabbatical from Berkeley Divinity School at Yale in Spring and Summer of 2020. I thank the trustees of the School, and Dean Gregory Sterling of Yale Divinity School, for the opportunity. They have not been preached as such, but formed as responses to the events of that year, including the illness of my father, Brian McGowan, in whose company they were written, the first preacher I knew and to whom I owe more than words can hope to say.

I am very grateful to David Clowney and Matthew Clowney for their generous provision of images from the work of the late Bettina Clowney.

I

CREATION and CROSS

†

Prologue

Each evangelist offers a similar account of what Jesus did on the cross, but a somewhat distinctive account of what he said. This devotion based on the seven sayings gleaned from the different narratives thus embodies the character of the gospel and the Gospels—a diversity appropriate to the variety of human experience, and a commonality appropriate to the depth of human need.

Seven sayings. The medieval Christians who first excerpted and counted them thus doubtless saw something in this number itself. Sevens occur across Scripture and tradition as significant groups and sequences; seven gifts of the Spirit, seven virtues and vices, seven days of creation not least. Of these seven sayings the great Franciscan theologian St Bonaventure said:

I Creation and Cross

> Our Vine uttered seven words while he was raised upon the cross. They are, as it were, seven leaves that are ever green. Or if you prefer, your Bridegroom can be thought of as a kind of lute, which is an instrument that consists of a piece of wood shaped like a cross. His body, in place of the strings, is stretched across the wood, but the seven words are the individual strings (*Vitis Mystica*).[1]

Other medieval commentators drew parallels between the seven words from the cross and seven wounds sustained by Jesus—counting them as the four nail piercings, the crown of thorns, the lash, and the spear.

But the seven days and acts of creation invite particular comparison and reflection with these words. Each of Jesus's seven words from the cross can be understood as a creative act, as a new divine work. In the narrative of Genesis chapter 1, God also creates by utterance seven times: "let there be . . ." Here too, Jesus—the divine creative Word made flesh—speaks, and the world is made anew.

The idea that Jesus does anything on the cross is remarkable, because of the nature of a cross. A cross of course is for suffering; but in particular it was designed for immobility, constraint, and passivity. The anguish of the cross was, as much as or more than the agony of the nails, a matter of being prevented from acting, being rendered an object and not a subject, becoming a mere thing to be acted upon.

And yet this cross is for us Jesus's great work, his creative masterpiece. More than any miraculous exercise of power over nature or human infirmity recorded in the Gospels, more than any profound teaching we have from him in longer

---

1. Bonaventure, *The Mystical Vine: A Treatise on the Passion of Our Lord*, Fleur de Lys Series (Riverside, IL: Akenside Press, 2016), 39.

1 Creation and Cross

and challenging words than these, it is this story, this time and place, where he does his greatest work. Bound and nailed tight, he remakes the world and us, and as in the beginning, creates by word.

ONE

*Then Jesus said, "Father, forgive them;
for they do not know what they are doing."*

Jesus gets the hardest work done first, we might say, with the first word. "Father, forgive them." A man has just been nailed to a cross by violent occupiers, and is being jeered at by his compatriots. A few words of resistance or judgment, of foreshadowed comeuppance, might not have made us think much less of Jesus. He was capable of such frankness, after all: "Woe to you scribes," and so on. But this is not what we find here.

Rather, as Luke (and he alone) tells us, Jesus begins his saving work with "Father, forgive." And note that it is not just some general magnanimity either; he says "Father forgive them, for they do not know what they are doing." Well, they actually seem to know pretty well exactly what they are doing, in the usual terms; the trials of Jesus, his appearances before colonial and local authorities across the preceding day, have involved numerous points at which the various perpetrators, active and passive alike, could have stopped the momentum

I   Creation and Cross

of violence. In our terms, they were intent and malign, and knew just what they were doing.

This is not, however, just a sort of overweaning kindness on Jesus's part. In fact in another, deeper sense, they do not know what they are doing, for they have mistaken who he is; as St Paul says, "none of the rulers of this world knew [this hidden mystery which God foreordained before the ages for his glory], for if they had known, they would not have crucified the Lord of glory" (1 Cor 2:7–8).

What Paul hints at here is that they do not know what God is doing in Christ and on the cross. Doing this, what they think they are doing—keeping order by making an example of a trouble-maker—becomes in fact another sort of thing. They are the unwitting co-workers with Jesus in this labor of forgiving the world; and he blesses them, movingly, strikingly, by including them explicitly, even and specifically his enemies, in the scope of God's extraordinary mercy. For of course he came to forgive those—all of us—whose actions have made these events take place. "Forgive them." Forgive *us*.

Forgiveness is hard work, work that we often find beyond our powers. This example may seem beyond us to emulate. And some early Christians regarded Jesus as stretching forgiveness beyond the bounds of good taste with this saying; there were many ancient manuscripts of Luke's Gospel from which this verse was omitted, probably excised by scribal correctors who (as such so often do) thought they knew the mind of God better than Jesus did, or at least than Luke did. It is the only one of these seven sayings that has been subject to such treatment, and therefore apparently the hardest to accept and make sense of. The objection may have been sharpened by the difficult relationships between Christians and

Jews in the early centuries; the idea of forgiveness for those labeled Jesus's enemies in particular seemed unpalatable. But this saying stands in its significance, and in its authenticity too.

We must accept that God's forgiveness does not work according to our sensibilities. Here at the cross, even the cruel and the vile are offered the reality of a divine embrace that we simply cannot comprehend. And if it is hard to accept that God's forgiveness extends to those whom we despise and blame for our own ills and the world's, it is or should be as hard and as important to know that we ourselves are included in it. In the end, we may not need so much or only to comprehend how inexplicably wide God's mercy is for others, but to understand, little by little, that God's mercy has comprehended us.

TWO

*He replied, "Truly I tell you,
today you will be with me in Paradise."*

Jesus from the cross remakes the world by Word, as in the beginning God makes all things. In the first saying from the cross, Jesus shouldered the difficult burden of forgiveness, praying for his tormentors. In the second word of his seven, his creative voice draws back from the audience of the jeering crowds to the strange intimacy of a conversation between three dying men.

While the mockery of Jesus by onlookers and/or his fellow-sufferers is reported in all the Gospels, Luke's version analyzes the action more finely:

> One of the criminals [Luke never calls them "thieves" interestingly—their crimes are not specified] who were hanged there kept deriding him and saying, "Are you not the Messiah? Save yourself and us!" But the other rebuked him, saying, "Do you not fear God, since you are under the same sentence of condemnation? And we indeed have been condemned justly, for

I Creation and Cross

> we are getting what we deserve for our deeds, but this man has done nothing wrong." Then he said, "Jesus, remember me when you come into your kingdom." He replied, "Truly I tell you, today you will be with me in Paradise." (Luke 23:39–43)

Paradise. The Israelites borrowed the word from their Persian neighbors and one-time overlords; it refers to a walled pleasure-garden, such as ancient near Eastern rulers might have enjoyed, and which most of their subjects could only have imagined or peeked into. The word occurs a few times in the Old Testament; in the Song of Songs for instance the lover calls his beloved "a garden enclosed," and a "paradise" of pomegranates.

And yes, a paradise is also that sort of place depicted in the Genesis creation story of the first humans, that famous Garden of Eden, a park where "out of the ground the Lord God made to grow every tree that is pleasant to the sight and good for food" (Gen 2:9). To be in Paradise is to hear God walking in the garden in the cool of the evening, to be in the presence of the tree of life, to be naked and not ashamed.

There is no starker contrast with the Golgotha experienced by these crucified men, deprived of all food, drink, and care of any kind, bodies hung as strange fruit on trees of death, and naked, not innocently but stripped and exposed for the sake of shame and degradation.

The strangely faith-filled criminal asked to be remembered in Jesus's kingdom, but Jesus's response is that he will be with him in Paradise. Jesus brings these two things, kingdom and Paradise, together.

The whole of the Gospel has been full of the preaching of a kingdom by Jesus, the kingdom of God. He has told

He replied, "Truly I tell you, today you will be with me in Paradise."

parables that explain what it is like, taught his disciples to pray for it to come, embodied in his own actions the kingly authority of justice and love that mark this true ruler of Israel, a new Davidic king. This kingdom proclaimed by Jesus was a future hope, an end of all things, the point towards which human history was going, where the justice and love of God would be made real, and which Jesus's followers hoped—and hope still—his arrival and his mission had inaugurated, an end of suffering, but an end.

So Jesus answers the criminal's desire for the kingdom with a promise of Paradise, offering an assurance of God's love that goes beyond death, and that is available even to the least likely of us. But he does so by drawing the hope for the end and the remembrance of the beginning together in his body on the cross as one thing, creating Paradise from Golgotha, a garden out of what sounds, from its name, like a barren rocky outcrop. So the promise to the criminal and to us is not only of assurance of God's love beyond death at the end, but that the end is the whole creation renewed, a vision of humankind and the natural order restored to the beauty of that ancient garden.

One man jeered at Jesus and asked, if he were the Messiah, the Davidic king, to get them down from the cross. Another man asks to be remembered in Jesus's messianic kingdom. We know nothing else about these two and why one speaks so differently from the other; but Jesus's promise to the latter is, because he asks for it, that he has the chance to go back; to go back, as though to begin again, to shed the burden of his life's pain and wrongdoing, and to be renewed like the flowers of a garden that come again each year mysteriously.

I   Creation and Cross

We know nothing of his life, but we do know our own. How many of us do not long to go back, before "that thing" happened, or "that decision" was made? How many of us do not wish to go back and begin again, to have that fresh start and not to bear the consequences of things done by ourselves and others? There are things each of us wishes had never happened, and things that we wish had; things done and left undone, our own and others'. Jesus offers this possibility without the necessity of erasing all that has happened to us, without pretending that these things are not part of our reality any more than he pretends the criminal's life is not his own. The possibility of Paradise comes again and again, not just at the beginning.

In George Herbert's poem from *The Temple* called "The Flower," he muses on the human condition and life before God, considering how our own experiences of spiritual bloom and blight need not be avoided or denied, but educate us about that first and final garden:

> These are thy wonders, Lord of love,
> To make us see we are but flowers that glide:
> Which when we once can finde and prove,
> Thou hast a garden for us, where to bide.[1]

We need not shed our experience to come into this kingdom that is Paradise. At the center of this Paradise into which we are invited stands the cross, now a tree of life, and Jesus borne on it offering us this garden "where to bide also," however late we ask for his kingdom and to be remembered in it.[2]

---

1. George Herbert, *The Poems of George Herbert* (Oxford: H. Frowde, at Oxford University Press, 1913), 172.

2. See further on this theme Christopher Irvine, *The Cross and Creation in*

He replied, "Truly I tell you, today you will be with me in Paradise."

Sixth-century poet Venantius Fortunatus helps us glimpse this divine joining of beginning and end, Golgotha and Paradise:

> Faithful Cross, above all other,
> one and only noble Tree,
> none in foliage, none in blossom,
> none in fruit thy peer may be;
> sweet the wood, and sweet the iron,
> and thy load, most sweet is he.³

Liturgy and Art (London: SPCK, 2013).

3. As translated by J. M. Neale; Elon Foster, ed., *Cyclopaedia of Poetry: Embracing the Best from All Sources and on All Subjects* (New York: T. Y. Crowell & Company, 1876), 143.

THREE

When Jesus saw his mother and the disciple whom he loved standing beside her, he said to his mother, "Woman, here is your son." Then he said to the disciple, "Here is your mother." And from that hour the disciple took her into his own home.

In the Basilica of Saint Clare in Assisi there hangs a famous cross, a Byzantine-style painted crucifix of the eleventh century and not much less than life-size, which had once been in another local Church, that of San Damiano. By the thirteenth century, San Damiano had already fallen into disrepair when a young Francesco de Bernadone, taking shelter there one day, believed the cross spoke to him. "Rebuild my Church," Francis heard this image of the crucified Jesus say; and being somewhat literal-minded, he took the Lord to be calling for repair work on that very building, and sure enough undertook it. Francis and his followers however came to understand that word from the cross more profoundly over the

I Creation and Cross

following years. It had not been so much about renovation projects as about living stones, and about love; it was a call to build community, the community of the church.

The San Damiano crucifix is a busy sort of cross. Unlike those of the later centuries, presenting only Jesus's suffering body more or less realistically, that crucifix at Assisi is a flat, crossed-shaped painting depicting a veritable crowd, figures painted beside and around Jesus, down the length and along the arms of the cross. Angels and apostles squeeze their ways into the gaps beside and beneath him. It is a crucifix that depicts not just Jesus, but the world he is remaking, a world of renewed relationships, a community.

Like many others, this cross gives prominence to the recipients of this third creative word from the cross, that is, to the mother of Jesus and the disciple whom Jesus loved, to give those whom we know as Mary and John their designations from John's Gospel, standing next to Jesus. When Francis heard the San Damiano crucifix speaking to him and instructing him, he may also have been recalling this more ancient word from the first cross and those to whom it was delivered, depicted on the one in front of him.

"Woman, behold your son. Son, behold your mother" is a breathtakingly simple creation of relationship. With this third word of his new creation from the cross, Jesus makes a family of two who loved him as much as any ever have, but who were not otherwise bound to each other before. In acting thus, he effectively founds the church, a community of love based on love of him.

Jesus's creative work on the cross is not only that of offering forgiveness and the hope of Paradise; it is also the work of restoring us as human beings to one other. Sin—the human experience of brokenness and failure—is not only a matter of our distance from God, but of our mutual alienation.

A work of salvation that seemed to remedy our individual needs for forgiveness and healing would be meaningless, were it not to extend to healing the brokenness of human community. All those in this city today going about their business outside the walls of this church, however little explicit sense of God or of awareness of the spiritual character of the human malaise they may have, would be hard pressed to deny the reality of our humanity itself being broken.

Each generation, each year, seems to have its distinctive ways of being inhuman; take your pick today between racism and terrorism, insurgencies far away and surging inequality close to home, or just consider our squabbles over which of our inhumanities is really the worst, and which remedy for it the least vile.

But we need not look to the easy pickings of politics to ponder the scope of human brokenness. In the realities of our own everyday lives, we discover again and again how hard it is simply to be loving, how hard merely to be kind; so even in our families, our friendships, our churches, we experience—and cause—brokenness in relationship, and we may feel angry and alone, and cause others to feel so too.

In the narrative of Genesis, where the origins of the world and humankind are narrated theologically through the collective mythic memory of Israel, we often speak of a single "fall," when Adam and Eve are expelled from the Garden of Eden. In fact there are multiple falls across that primeval narrative, people falling away from each other as well as from God; Cain's and Abel's violent sundering of brotherhood, the Tower of Babel's story of humanity scattered into fragmentary parts of mutual incomprehension, are signs of the human condition as much as is the story of our failure to stay in relationship with God in Paradise.

In all those stories, humans are unable to love those to whom they were already bound by blood; but in this one, Jesus binds together those who had no such tie before. Where once we struggled to love those whom love us, Jesus suggests we can love others we had not known or understood, even our enemies; and more to the point, he creates that love in the speaking of it.

If we dare follow him as far as the cross we can expect him to speak to us, as to Mary and John, as to Francis. We can expect him to make us mothers and sons of people we did not expect, and probably did not want. Jesus will not exempt the refugee and the migrant from his care and our responsibility in the name of our own security, for instance. Nor will he exempt those closest at hand, whom we have found ourselves unable to remain in relationship with, because we cannot understand or do not like their opinions or values or identity.

As he speaks still from the cross, we hear not only his binding of Mary and John but of ourselves, to each other and to him. "Rebuild my Church"; "rebuild my world." Now today, when as we go out into the streets of the city, he says again and again "here," "here," "here"; "here is your father," "here is your daughter," "brother," "sister," "son," "mother."

†

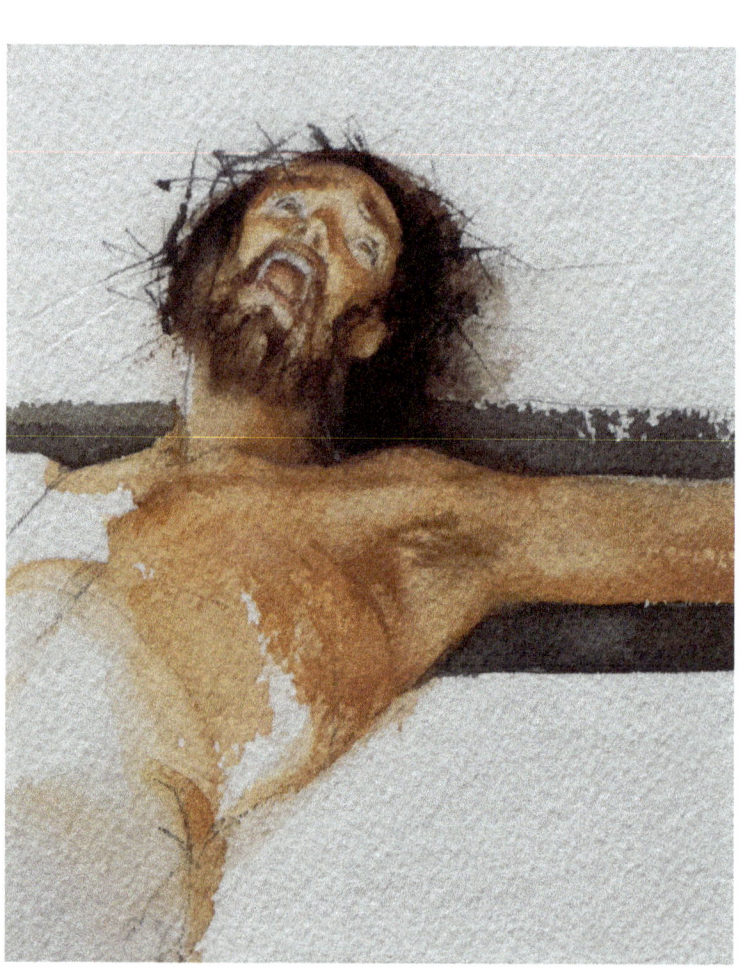

FOUR

"My God, my God, why have you forsaken me?"

This is the only saying from the cross recorded in two of the Gospels—Mark, apparently the earliest, and Matthew, which follows it closely. And it is the only saying from the cross in either of these Gospels. It is a bleak, a desperate call—the mid-point as well as the low point of these seven sayings.

I have been speaking of Jesus as working from the cross, saving and re-creating our humanity by his seven words; this is of course at all points a paradox, as the helpless Galilean's life and power drains away. At this point however, having spoken of forgiveness, and of Paradise, and of love, Jesus seems to fall away from his creative restorative work, and lets his brokenness speak out.

Jesus is of course quoting Scripture; if we objected to the possibility that Jesus really experienced desolation, we could some might take reassurance from the fact that even a dying Jesus can summon up the presence of mind and strength of body—and theological education—to recite Psalm 22. This,

I Creation and Cross

however, is not what I think we should hear first and foremost in this wrenching cry of despair. We do him and ourselves no favors to make Jesus a pious hypocrite in order to protect our assumptions about him. We should assume that he meant what he said; that he believed God had forsaken him, and that his call was made in despair.

This is the moment where the reality of the cross cuts the deepest, not just in terms of Jesus's physical anguish and the sense of life falling away; these are the fate of us all. What cuts most deeply here is Jesus's realization that all the creativity of his ministry, all the hope of the kingdom, all the power of God to heal and save, all the love, is in this moment gone. It is not the Romans who are the problem at this moment, not the chief priests and the scribes, not the fallible disciples, nor stray family members who need accommodation; it is God. God is the problem.

There seems, then, little that is creative about this fourth word, even if he gives voice to moments of doubt that we must all feel. I beg however to differ from my own proposal so far; this is a moment of creation. In fact, this is that moment when the creative work begun with the incarnation and the word of an angel, decades before, reaches its completion.

Occasionally Good Friday falls on what would have been the Feast of the Annunciation, were it not that our calendrical rule in the Western church prevents such a concurrence, and moves Lady Day to the week after the Easter Octave.[1] The Eastern church has no such rule; a very busy liturgical schedule simply becomes ever more crowded. This concurrence has happened a few times in recent years, but will not again during any of our lifetimes (unforeseen progress in

---

1. This was the case when this sermon was delivered in 2016.

"My God, my God, why have you forsaken me?"

medical science notwithstanding). I call it a "concurrence," rather than coincidence, deliberately. There were those in the ancient church who dated the crucifixion to this day in the solar calendar as well. Although there was no strict historical basis for this, some suggested that March 25, which could have been Passover the year of Jesus's death, would have been a likely date, years before, for the incarnation itself. The years of Jesus's life thus would have formed a whole, announced by an angel to his mother and given up to the Father on the same day, reflecting divine purpose in the calendar.[2]

One year this took place was 1608, when John Donne famously wrote about the concurrence, pondering Mary's place at both events:

> She sees Him nothing twice at once, who's all;
> She sees a Cedar plant itself and fall,
> Her Maker put to making, and the head
> Of life at once not yet alive yet dead;
> She sees at once the virgin mother stay
> Reclused at home, public at Golgotha;
> Sad and rejoiced she's seen at once, and seen
> At almost fifty and at scarce fifteen;
> At once a Son is promised her, and gone;
> Gabriel gives Christ to her, He her to John . . .[3]

That concurrence is perhaps the clue to what is most truly and starkly conveyed in Jesus's cry of despair. The real humanity assumed in Mary was not just God dressing up to

---

2. Andrew McGowan, "How December 25 Became Christmas," *Bible Review* 18, no. 6 (December 2002), 46.

3. Robert Anderson, ed., *The Poetical Works of Dr John Donne*, The Works of the British Poets: With Prefaces, Biographical and Critical 4 (London: John & Arthur Arch et al., 1795), 44.

I Creation and Cross

look like one of us, while retaining divinity as a protection against what humanity really entails.

Before he died the Roman Emperor Vespasian is said by Suetonius to have joked "Oh dear, I think I am becoming a god" (*Vesp.* 23.4). Here Jesus says, "O God, I think I have become human."

At this point, with this cry of despair, Jesus knows he is going to die, as we all will, and faces the horror of this honestly. And as much or more than this, as much a mark of our humanity as mere mortality, it is the loss of hope; for if he can remain confident of his salvation, if death were merely to be a nap for Jesus, he would not really be one of us. If Jesus is to be saved, it must now be by power of the God hidden from him, not by anything that remains in him. And so it is for us; at death, we trust not in some innate ability to drift on as immortal souls, but in the power of the one who on the third day might raise Jesus again.

What is created in this fourth word from the cross, the "let there be" of it, is the same word spoken by the angel, or the end of a sentence begun decades before. On the face of it they are contradictory. Gabriel says to Mary, "The Lord is with you." Jesus says "Lord, why have you left me?" But the issue is the same. Is God with us or not? Only if Jesus is truly human—only if he can experience mortality and abandonment—can we say God is with is. And only if God has forsaken Jesus—allowed him into the reality of sin and death which grips us all—can he then be truly with us, and free us from them. This is the mystery of the incarnation; the Word not merely spoken, but made flesh.

†

FIVE

After this, when Jesus knew that all was now finished, he said (in order to fulfill the scripture), "I am thirsty."

In the Gospel of John from which this fifth word comes, Jesus is not so much a passive victim on the cross, but remains in charge. John the evangelist presents this statement as a deliberate, even a calculated one; "he said *in order to fulfill the scripture*, 'I am thirsty.'" For John, the cross is Jesus's moment of triumph—in this Gospel Jesus had, long before when speaking with the curious Nicodemus, said that "just as Moses lifted up the serpent in the wilderness, so must the Son of Man be lifted up, that whoever believes in him may have eternal life" (John 3:14); later Jesus also says, "I, when I am lifted up from the earth, will draw all to myself" (John 12:32). So the cross for the Fourth Gospel is not failure or abandonment, nor merely a necessary if unpleasant step on the way to something else; it is here that Jesus triumphs.

So the statement "I thirst" is prefaced carefully by John with this note that Jesus spoke "in order to fulfill the

I Creation and Cross

scripture"—not, in other words, merely to reflect the incidental needs of the tortured body, but to achieve something, to accomplish and to create. This fifth word of Jesus's new creation from the cross arises from human need, but illustrates divine purpose.

What follows his statement needs to be read as well: "A jar full of sour wine was standing there. So they put a sponge full of the wine on a branch of hyssop and held it to his mouth" (John 19:29).

The Scripture in question that had to be fulfilled is not actually stated, and not otherwise completely clear. Jesus is usually taken to be referring to Psalm 69, which states "for my thirst they gave me vinegar to drink" or to Psalm 22, already quoted by him according to Mark and Matthew in that cry of abandonment, where it goes on to say:

> my mouth is dried up like a potsherd,
> and my tongue sticks to my jaws;
> you lay me in the dust of death (Ps 22:15).

The Psalmist provides many such pictures of the righteous sufferer who experiences pain and seeks God's vindication, expressing the depths of their own need while recalling and hoping for better times. Yet when John says that Jesus spoke to fulfill "scripture," those texts just mentioned may not be the only possibilities.

Jesus died at Passover. Each of the Synoptic Gospels—Matthew, Mark, and Luke—presents the famous story of Jesus eating and drinking with his friends a few hours earlier, the Last Supper, as a Passover seder in the stricter sense, including the actions of Jesus commemorating his coming death and (most clearly in Luke) committing its remembrance to

After this, when Jesus knew that all was now finished

us in the sacrament of the Eucharist. And each of three includes a vow of renunciation by Jesus, after drinking, of the fruit of the vine; as Luke puts it, "I tell you that from now on I shall not drink of the fruit of the vine until the kingdom of God comes" (Luke 22:18). Mark and Matthew also record an incident at the point of Jesus being crucified, where he is offered wine drugged with gall or myrrh as a sort of primitive anesthetic, but refuses it, presumably in the spirit of this vow of renunciation.

In the chronology John's Gospel presents, however, the main feast or Seder of the Passover has not yet taken place when Jesus is crucified. There may have been a difference in ancient reckoning of the feast day, and the evangelists take these different possibilities up in their portraits of the passion. For John, the Last Supper is a Passover meal only indirectly, placed around the time of the feast, but in fact slightly before it. While Jesus and his disciples celebrate a Last Supper together there is no reference to Jesus taking bread and wine as his body and blood, but instead emphasis is given to his taking off his outer garment and washing their feet. In John's Gospel the Passover strictly begins only when Jesus is already on the cross. Differences of historical reminiscence aside, what do we make of this?

It is not that the Passover is less important in this Gospel. Throughout John's Gospel the Passover, Israel's feast of liberation and renewal, plays an important part. The ministry of Jesus takes place across a cycle of Passovers and visits to Jerusalem for the feast. But Jesus has apparently been marked himself as a paschal lamb from a very early point; John the Baptizer refers to him at the beginning of the Gospel as the "Lamb of God who takes away the sin of the world" (John

I Creation and Cross

1:29), identifying Jesus as a lamb who will free his people from sin and death.

This last Passover is the fateful one where the identity of Jesus as lamb of God is revealed in its deepest sense; not as in the other Gospels, via him participating in the paschal lamb of the feast with his friends, but by becoming the lamb himself. In John, Pilate's sentence of condemnation had been issued at the time the paschal lambs were being slaughtered in the Jerusalem Temple in readiness for the feast that night, which was after Jesus has been taken down from the cross. As he hangs on the cross, this process of slaughter continues, and the preparations for the formal banquet, the seder, of the coming evening are being made.

Jesus's thirst then, is part of his fulfillment of this extraordinary feast, the fateful Passover. Jesus has eaten and drunk festively throughout his ministry, earning himself elsewhere the designation as a "glutton and a drunkard." Jesus, saying "I am thirsty," acts true to form, and now inaugurates the feast as he gives himself as food and drink for the world, fulfilling the command to keep the Passover in his body, and with his body. He fulfills Scripture not just by alluding to particular verses of the Psalms, but in keeping the feast committed to the Israelites of old in Scripture. He inaugurates the feast, as a seder is begun even now, with the cup of liberation. It comes to him not in a silver chalice but in a sponge on a hyssop branch, not a sweet and rich vintage well-paired to the feast but the sour wine of the everyday diet of the poor; but with it nonetheless he keeps his Passover feast, and shows himself to be the Lamb of God.

Saying "I am thirsty" and drinking, Jesus fulfills scripture, not only in evoking the Psalmist's bitterness and need,

After this, when Jesus knew that all was now finished

but in revealing the whole story of Scripture which has led from creation to exodus, in fulfilling the ordinance to keep the paschal feast, calling into being the great paschal feast. This act in the Fourth Gospel is his eucharistic institution, his sharing with us of himself. As he drinks, Christ our Passover has been sacrificed for us; let us celebrate the feast.

SIX

*When Jesus had received the wine,
he said, "It is finished."*

On the sixth day of creation in the Genesis account, God calls forth living creatures into being to populate the earth, beasts and cattle; God then makes humankind according to God's likeness. Then the narrator says:

> God saw everything that he had made, and indeed, it was very good. And there was evening, and there was morning, the sixth day. (Gen 1:31)

As in the sixth day of creation, Jesus with his sixth word from the cross reaches the point where all has been accomplished. He has done what was necessary, from beginning to end, from the angel's word to Mary, to journeys taken through Bethlehem and Galilee, to Samaria and the Decapolis, and even to Jerusalem the great city. He has taught and he has healed; he has sought out the lost and consoled the broken; he has spoken truth to power and to the powerless, offering

I Creation and Cross

the light of God's truth into places and to people darkened by sin and despair.

Consummatum est—it is finished. The meaning of this statement is not so much that something is over, but that is has been brought to completion, fruition, or that it has reached a goal. It is like the divine creative statement, a blessing in effect, on the sixth day—"God saw everything that he had made, and indeed, it was very good."

What has been accomplished? Jesus's life and ministry indeed, but also the whole scheme of creation and salvation.

John Donne, in that poem reflecting on the concurrence of Annunciation and Good Friday in 1608, puts it thus:

> All this, and all between, this day hath shown,
> The abridgement of Christ's story, which makes one
> (As in plain maps, the furthest west is east)
> Of the Angels' Ave and Consummatum est.[1]

But what has Jesus actually done, and why? Why has all this been necessary? What difference does this cross in particular make? It is a question more and more Christians have asked during the twentieth and twenty-first centuries, finding themselves unconvinced or even disturbed by some articulations of the doctrine of the atonement. In crudest form, there are those who say that Jesus died to assuage the Father's wrath, as a substitute for us in receiving a penalty otherwise due to humankind. At its worst this "penal substitution" view becomes the idea God is a cosmic psychopath, determined to kill his own son because of rules God will not break. This view we must reject firmly—not because it is distasteful to us, but because it is not true to the gospel.

---

1. Robert Anderson, ed., *The Poetical Works of Dr John Donne*, 44.

When Jesus had received the wine, he said, "It is finished."

All this does not mean that we do not need a doctrine of the atonement, as some would go so far as to say. This is merely to misunderstand what atonement is, or to hand it over to the caricatures of some fundamentalisms. We need atonement, because we need God, and we need forgiveness, and we need liberation from sin and death.

Jesus does not have to die because of a vengeful God, but because of a broken world. God did not kill Jesus, people did. Jesus suffers because of human inhumanity as so many still do today, in the spectacular results of war or gun violence, as well as in the often-unnoticed deaths of the lonely, the addicted, and the marginalized. A cross is at first glance—and at second—no more a thing to celebrate than a gun or a dirty syringe or an explosive belt; but a man on the cross in whom we see God is another matter.

The whole work of Christ, from incarnation to cross and beyond, is necessary because of the depth of sin and brokenness that is the human condition. In Genesis, God creates by word; in the Gospel the creative Word becomes flesh and dwells among us. In Christ, humankind is remade, and we find in him both a model for life but more importantly we encounter the reality of God entering human existence and re-creating what has been broken. The pattern for this is not divine violence or vengeance, but divine love and gift.

The key to God's saving work is that God enters fully into human reality, and redeems it by participating fully in it, across the full extent of our condition, as St Gregory Nazianzen put it: "What [he has not] assumed has not been healed; it is what is united to his divinity that is saved" (*Ep.* 101). This means the whole of life, from beginning to end, conception and birth, growth in personhood and learning, but also

1 Creation and Cross

vulnerability and mortality. God's completed creation is the recapitulation in Jesus of human life as intended, in all ways like us but without sin (cf. Heb 4:15). This life becomes an example to us of course, but not merely an example; that alone would merely underline our frailty and failure, for we do not and cannot live as he did merely by the power of a good example. Our hope lies in the fact that in Christ God was reconciling the world to himself (2 Cor 5:19) and that his life changes all life. Placing our hope in him, baptized into his death, we participate in him and his renewed human reality.

What is completed on the cross is this full and complete self-giving of God. What was once created is now re-created.

SEVEN

Then Jesus, crying with a loud voice, said, "Father, into your hands I commend my spirit." Having said this, he breathed his last.

Jesus's labor completed on the cross, like that of God in creation, gives way to a time of rest. What comes next, in Gospel as in Genesis, is the Sabbath.

"And on the seventh day," Genesis says, "God finished the work that he had done, and he rested on the seventh day from all the work that he had done. So God blessed the seventh day and hallowed it, because on it God rested from all the work that he had done in creation." So God "finished" the work he had done on that seventh day, the Sabbath—even though it was on the previous day, the sixth, that God already "saw everything that he had made, and it was good." What then remained to be done on the seventh, or could be done, that amounted to "finishing"?

Creation, it seems, was not complete in the making alone; the last thing, the Sabbath itself, was the very fact of creation existing in its completeness before God. On the Sabbath,

I Creation and Cross

God and creation enjoy the reality of what has been made, and the fact of being related as creator and creation. This is now the finished work. The point of creation was not just the divine sovereignty manifest in the making in the six days, and the divine "let there be," but the relationship that is its result; God's creation is not merely a task, but a state of being. And God blesses that result, in and on the Sabbath rest.

So what is created on the Sabbath is that time itself, that rest, which celebrates the fact of creation and makes its enjoyment, rather than activity for its own sake, the goal of life.

As Jesus dies he enters the Sabbath literally, as Friday draws on to a close. St Augustine of Hippo suggested that the rest of Jesus in death between this time and the first day of the week was his observance of Sabbath, like that given by God in Genesis and in the Law of Moses, and that the interval between his death and resurrection reflects his observance of the Sabbath according to law.[1] To have risen before that would have been to work, and to defile the Sabbath. So even in death Jesus will be fulfilling the law, complete in his obedience to the God of creation.

The rest of Jesus in death is therefore not about passivity. Having worked on the cross, Jesus now rests, as the Creator rested on the Sabbath, to bless and enjoy what has been made, because Jesus's work too is done, and the failed and broken creation is renewed by his embodied word: forgiven, loved, redeemed, and more, and he himself now fully a part of what he had both made and remade, not despite his death but in it.

Although there will be a further day, an eighth day of creation as the ancient Christians saw it, when Jesus will see new life, this Sabbath rest is not to be passed by lightly as a

---

1. See Augustine, *Contra Faustum* 16.29.

mere hiatus. Human existence is so often frenetic activity or unceasing labor; we tire of meaningless work and the world itself groans under our efforts to sustain ourselves. As Ecclesiastes says:

> What do mortals get from all the toil and strain with which they toil under the sun? For all their days are full of pain, and their work is a vexation; even at night their minds do not rest. (Eccl 2:22–3)

Although we must work to live and, properly understood, our work can be a contribution to God's continuing work in creation, there is a sense in which we are all seeking a rest beyond our present labors. All our work and all our quests are truly oriented towards this rest, whether we know it or not. Augustine again said, "you [Lord] have made us for yourself and our heart is restless until it rests in you" (*Conf.* 1.1). Jesus also anticipates this desire for rest during his ministry, saying "Come to me, all you that labor and are heavy laden, and I will give you rest" (Matt 11:28).

So as Jesus breathes his last and is taken to his Sabbath rest, we too find ourselves praying for true rest; not merely the end of labor, but the opportunity to enjoy its fruit. The literal Sabbath that many in this city will observe in a few hours is a sign of that deeper Sabbath that is both embedded in the good creation, and now for us restored in a new creation; what God has done, once and again and still today, is very good, and blessed. That rest is a truth in our present life, and a hope for our future; for the end of pain and suffering, and for the fulfillment of hope and love.

At the end of Bach's great St John Passion, a lullaby is sung as Jesus is taken to the tomb, for him but also for us: *Ruht wohl, ruht wohl, ihr heilige Gebeine;*

I Creation and Cross

Rest well, rest well, you sacred limbs,
I will weep for you no more
rest well, and bring me also to rest.

II

CONVERSATIONS at the CROSS

†

Prologue

In the previous set of reflections, I considered Jesus's own words at the cross, as preachers have long done, looking for connections between them, and between them and the rest of the words of Scripture. Yet there are other words spoken at the cross, and other people who speak them. Some of these are alluded to or reported indirectly in the Gospels, but only a few are recorded verbatim. And there are other people present at the cross, or inextricably linked to Jesus's presence there, whose speech at other times and places resonates around the scene even if not spoken there, illuminating the cross itself or being interpreted by it. And sometimes these absences or silences speak louder than words.

II Conversations at the Cross

So the mockers and the traitors are given a voice in the story along with the faithful few and those waiting to see what will happen next, and some perhaps representative group of these are gathered here, in a second set of seven—or almost seven—words, not *from* the cross but *to* the cross, and to the crucified. They necessarily represent the variety of responses to Jesus, who in and after death was no more simply or universally received and heard than in life.

These seven have been chosen not merely to gather all the statements reported by the Gospels at the crucifixion, or to present the onlookers as representative figures, but more specifically to glean responses to the other and more famous seven uttered by Jesus himself. Thus while two sayings are drawn immediately from the scene, another is from the wider Passion Narrative, a few have been imported from other points in the Gospels, and one is not speech but silence. They are the other part of a dialogue that is ongoing. As the original seven words offer both a unity and diversity of sorts, so too do these; the range of human—and divine—responses reflect what the cross leaves in its wake, but their unity subsists in the fact that the eternal Word not only speaks, but listens too.

†

ONE

Judas

"Surely not I, Rabbi?" (Matt 26:25)

Despite the Savior of the world setting an example with his own first word from the cross—"Father, forgive them"—Christians themselves are not so free in forgiving. Forgiveness is hard, for one thing. It certainly sounds like a good idea; yet the reality of forgiveness has to be tested concretely, rather than as mere principle. In Matthew's Gospel, Peter probes this question revealingly, asking how many times he should forgive a brother, and apparently thinking seven was a pretty generous number that would earn him some credit (Matt 18:21–2). Not so, it turns out. And this impulse to constrain the fearful possibility of forgiveness on the loose continues.

We can see all around us today, and across history, evidence of Christians personally and institutionally trying to plug the leaks in this awkward boat of radical forgiveness to which they have been consigned, testing the conditions that can or must be attached to forgiveness, the limits that must be established, and so on. And often it's not Peter's quantitative test they are trying to cope with, it's the qualitative one: how bad does something have to be, before I actually don't have to forgive it?

The acid test case for thinking about forgiveness must be Judas, who got us into this mess in the first place. What will we say of him? Jesus, in the text we have received as the first word from the cross, solves the problem fairly clearly, however hesitant we may be to accept it: "Father, forgive them" is clearly a reference to those responsible for his suffering and death in particular. No, there isn't really anything worse to forgive than this. It's not that we all have the capacity to emulate Jesus here or otherwise, of course. And even Jesus wasn't condoning torture and killing, which can never be condoned whoever is doing the suffering. He was pointing past them to the fact that it is always people, real human beings, who do the worst imaginable things. The suffering they cause will end, but the people themselves remain available for us to forgive, or not, afterwards.

The church has of course set a poor example by denying the meaning of the saying in a quite specific way. The historic attribution of guilt to the Jewish people was the great and fatal historic exception of Christian ethics, the avoidance of the obvious concrete challenge of forgiveness in favor of the abstract principle, and hence applying it selectively in ways that suited our preconceptions.

The anti-Semitic exception to any expectation of forgiveness was even facilitated by the name of "Judas," or Judah, who is indeed, by name at least, the paradigmatic Judean or

Jew. The controversy about whether Jesus's saying about forgiveness from the cross could even be accepted as part of the authentic text of Luke was closely related to whether or not early scribes and readers thought it referred to Jews ("surely not") or Romans ("what a relief").

More recently, scholarship has shifted the gaze of historic blame, correctly pointing to the fact that Roman law and authority was certainly the real cause of Jesus's death, and that "Jewish" complicity was merely that of certain elites. Even these accurate observations however seem to be fodder for the old wrong question, "whom shall I forgive?" Christians are now more likely—although not quite likely enough—to understand that a blood libel against the Jews is both historically false and theologically repugnant, but then the searchlight of blame seems to be readjusted rather than turned off. Arguing over just who it is that should be blamed, and who can thus be exempted from the forgiveness at the heart of the gospel, is rather to miss the point, but of course we often do that—hence a cross in the first place.

Judas remains in the frame in a unique way however, despite the lessening of the anti-Semitic trope. While some elite locals seem to have been more actively malicious towards Jesus, and Pilate far more powerful in sealing his fate, Judas has the unique taint of being one of those close to Jesus, a true believer, whose failure constitutes a unique threat. The traitor is a greater threat than the enemy.

Nevertheless, many have wondered from early times about the salvation of Judas. While medieval tradition has him as the epitome of evil, his role is presented in Scripture itself as more a necessary but tragic one, the result of external evil and not merely of his own choices.¹ Ancient Christian writers were thus at least somewhat sympathetic to his plight. Origen of Alexandria perceived there was a "mystery" there in Judas, something not readily reduced to jeers and accusations.² Origen even believed Judas experienced a genuine form of repentance after the fateful events—but that it was not quite enough.

The obvious and unhappy tendency to cast judgment on others, or to allow it to be cast, often says more about us and what we are hiding, even from ourselves. So too the problem with Judas may not simply be the enormity of his crime but, just as Origen thought, the limits to his own capacity to accept forgiveness. While unthinking moralism and rousing condemnation of the "sinners" (whoever they may be at a given time) is one side of Christians' incapacity to grasp the meaning of the cross, there is another aspect that initially seems like the opposite, but probably isn't. The most viciously judgmental, you may have noted, often use their high-minded condemnation to draw a veil over their own problems, even to themselves. This phenomenon, I suspect, lies underneath another famous but contested saying of Jesus about sin and forgiveness, namely that "the one without sin [should] cast the first stone" (John 8:7). This again seems to have given some Christian scribes the idea that Jesus was lowering the bar too far, and the story in which it was embedded thus travelled uncertainly in Gospel manuscripts.³

---

1. See further Felicity Harley, "Hanging by a Thread: The Death of Judas in Early Christian Art," in *The Eloquence of Art: Essays in Honour of Henry Maguire*, ed. Andrea Olsen Lam and Rossitza Schroeder (London: Routledge, 2020), 115–30.

2. See Origen, *Comm. on John* 32.21.

3. See Jennifer Knust and Tommy Wasserman, "Earth Accuses Earth:

Judas

Judas was not at the cross. One of the few sayings attributed to him however comes from just prior to these events, and seems to echo around when Jesus speaks his first word. When just hours before Jesus predicted his betrayal, Judas said "surely, Rabbi, not me?" Judas's incredulity, whether feigned or real at that point, seems to continue from here to his end. He moves from being unable to imagine the betrayal prediction as about him, to being unable to imagine the offer as forgiveness as for him. Is this not the case with us too, whether about forgiveness for ourselves or for others? The sheer unlikelihood of forgiveness, its being spoken from the cross under the most impossible of circumstances, evokes our deepest objections not only to Judas's forgiveness, but to our own. The reconstructed conversation between Jesus and Judas is thus one we may all have to acknowledge:

"Father, forgive them." "Surely, not I?"

Tracing What Jesus Wrote on the Ground," *The Harvard Theological Review* 103, no. 4 (2010), 407–46.

TWO

Dismas

"Jesus, remember me when you come into your kingdom." (Luke 23:42)

We don't really know why these two other men found their way to crosses next to Jesus, but there are clues, and they are uncomfortable ones. Luke uses the rather neutral "wrongdoers" to describe them, implying some sort of criminality. Mark and Matthew use a more pointed word for them, that could mean "robbers," but is perhaps better translated "insurrectionists." Crucifixion was used by the Romans for a variety of victims and purposes, so we cannot be sure, but rebels were subject to just this treatment, and the third man between them was certainly being crucified for exactly that reason.

Tradition has tried to give the two others more personal identities, making them subjects who could be distinguished by their behavior in this scene, rather than colored together and primarily by the reputations they brought to the cross.

II Conversations at the Cross

Sometimes in pious retellings they are called "Zoathan" and "Chammatha," or "Titus" and "Dumachus," but earliest and most commonly they are named "Dismas" and "Gestas."

The possibility that Dismas and Gestas were not merely burglars or swindlers, but people who used or threatened violence hoping to change society and make their world a better place, is not to be dismissed lightly. There are some further clues that encourage this thought. Remember that fourth criminal in the story who never made it to the cross was named Barabbas, the one whose freedom was sought by the crowd in Jesus's place; John's Gospel identified him with just the same word Matthew and Mark had used for the other two (John 18:40). Barabbas was certainly a rebel (Mark 15:7). The crop the Romans were to plant that day seems then to have been a political one, not merely rough justice. So we should probably imagine Dismas and Gestas as crucified for just the same reason that Jesus was, and that Barabbas might have been, namely as threats to Roman power, who were being presented as examples to the onlookers in this perverse thicket of pain. They all wanted a better world, and ended up in a worse one.

Just as a great deal depends on how we describe these two, so also it matters exactly how we listen to what they themselves say at the cross. Their exchanges with Jesus in Luke are the most explicit conversation that takes place in the whole crucifixion narrative. Matthew and Mark do record both of them attacking Jesus—the word used there would better be translated as "reproach" than (as more traditionally) "revile" or "taunt." That is, we should probably hear these two as failed idealists complaining at Jesus's failure to achieve his goals, rather than as thugs taking a last minute of pleasure from jeering at the suffering of another. This same possibility helps make sense of both the companions' cries to Jesus in Luke, which are elaborated to distinguish them. The first, Gestas, begs him to save them (even though Luke also calls this a rebuke, or worse), wondering bitterly why the messianic promise has come to this. Dismas of course chides his companion, but then asks for the lost promise to be fulfilled: "Jesus, remember me when you come in your kingdom."

We have no particular reason to think Dismas is only imagining some post-mortem existence when he asks to be remembered. This "kingdom" of Jesus is not a new topic, after all; Jesus has spoken continually of the promised kingdom, the kingdom of God, which is always implicitly contrasted with the reign of the Romans, and whose proclamation is the whole reason Jesus had been crowned with thorns and now hangs on the cross with the ironic title over his head.

Jesus had spoken of this kingdom and of its imminence, even that some now living would see it (Luke 9:27). He has taught his disciples to pray for it (Luke 11:2), and to strive for it (Luke 12:11), not to hope for it merely as a reward after life's laboring in the vineyard is done. In this kingdom oppression and want were to be overcome, and people would come from all the points of the compass to eat (Luke 13:29). Yet Jesus also said, "The kingdom of God is not coming with things that can be observed; nor will they say, 'Look, here it is!' or 'There it is!' For, in fact, the kingdom of God is among you" (Luke 17:20b–21).

Dismas shows remarkable faith by invoking the kingdom even here; the plea to be remembered in Jesus's kingdom, and by implication the belief even there and then on the cross that there still could even be such a thing, might even be the first half-formed confession of the resurrection. When Jesus promises Dismas something that sounds a little different—"Paradise"—and says it will be theirs today, we do understand that the kingdom is something that exists beyond our present experience and understanding of life, to be sure. Yet even Dismas had claimed that possibility in his question, when imagining a future kingdom that worked differently from Caesar's, a paradise whose trees bore sweeter fruit than these crosses, for healing of the nations and not for suffering. To affirm that reality does not merely defer the kingdom, but rather extends it.

In this conversation between two rebels, Jesus and Dismas together lay claim to a hope with no support from earthly power or evidence but in the power of God in and beyond death as well as life. And they find again in the exchange that just as one of them had said before, the kingdom is among us.

†

THREE

Mary

"Do whatever he tells you." (John 2:5).

The picture shared by all the Gospels of a group of Galilean women supporters present at Jesus's execution, while the inconstant male disciples have almost all shrunk into the shadows, resolves itself only in the Gospel of John so as to include Mary, "the mother of Jesus," although her name is never used in this Gospel.

When Jesus speaks from the cross to Mary, and then to the beloved disciple we usually identify as John, he uses an unusual form that has raised interpretive eyebrows for as long as the story has been read and told: "Woman." The only other place this turn of phrase was used by Jesus was in the story of the wedding at Cana, and again it was to "the mother of Jesus." While there is no infancy story in John, the Cana event is a beginning story, as this one is an end. There, the evangelist had said: "Jesus did this, the first of his signs, in Cana of Galilee, and revealed his glory; and his disciples believed in him" (John 2:11). Here, where the greatest of his signs is taking shape as Jesus draws the world to himself (John 3:14), we see what his glory turns out to be.

The address "woman" has sometimes been taken as an imperious or uncouth tone, as though it had the same resonances a modern English speaker would hear. That is unlikely to be the real force of this expression. The two stories where it appears help interpret each other, and the ways Mary is addressed and described.

The word *woman* appears only one other time, where in his long farewell discourse Jesus uses a parable to tell the disciples how they will experience his departure and death:

> When a woman is in labor, she has pain, because her hour has come. But when her child is born, she no longer remembers the anguish because of the joy of having brought a human being into the world. So you have pain now; but I will see you again, and your hearts will rejoice, and no one will take your joy from you. (John 16:21–22)

This passage is the only time John mentions a woman giving birth, although it is a parable told to interpret a death. While it has a meaning for any reader responding to Jesus, the significance of the story may actually be embodied in this one "woman," the acknowledged "mother" present at both marriage feast and cross, and whose identity is foregrounded by this description and address.[1]

She says nothing at the cross, but at Cana Mary had said something: she said "Do whatever he tells you." Nothing in

---

1. John Behr, *John the Theologian and His Paschal Gospel: A Prologue to Theology* (Oxford: Oxford University Press, 2019), 184–85.

John's Gospel is ever only what it seems, and while the immediate issue there seems to be the help Jesus will give with the catering, sometimes a feast is not just a feast, and Mary's word resounds well past that episode. "Do whatever he tells you" also reminds us quite directly of two other stories about Mary in Luke's Gospel. First there is the Annunciation, where Mary's response to being told something is about putting word into fact: "let it be to me according to your word" (Luke 1:38). And there is the story where a woman in the crowd who calls out to Jesus: "'Blessed is the womb that bore you, and the breasts that you sucked!' But he said, 'Blessed rather are those who hear the word of God and keep it!'" (Luke 11:27–28). Given what Luke has already told us about Mary, this is just as much a reference to her as was the first blessing from the crowd, but again it is about translating his word into deed.

All of these stories and sayings link obedience or listening and transformation; while they speak of "doing," the significance of doing what he says turns out not to be merely in the acts themselves. The blessing that Jesus offers in the doing lies in discovering that hearing and keeping what he tells us will change us, will make us who we really are, or will be. Mary does not say at Cana "do whatever he says" to reinforce his authority, so much as to signal that in doing what he says, we may find the world changing. With his own words our own water may be turned into wine as at Cana, new relationships formed as at the cross, our past selves changed into their true future forms. Jesus's answer to her at Cana had suggested that the time for doing that, his "hour," was still to come, so that when he uses the same expression at the cross addressing her, we are meant to remember her words, as well as his own. Now his hour has come.

II Conversations at the Cross

Given John's sense of time, where the divine reality of God's work in Jesus is always visible at any point in the story to those with eyes to see, the fact that Mary's statement is not made at the cross is only a provocation to thought; the wedding feast is always happening in the background of whatever Jesus does and says, and the cross is always present too, the completion and revelation, the glory of what he has always been doing and saying.

Doing what he tells us, we find ourselves transformed, as much or more as anything we act on outside ourselves is changed. When Mary and John hear him speak from the cross, they hear not so much a command but a new reality already spoken into being, that had already been promised at the beginning: "to all who received him, who believed in his name, he gave the power to become children of God" (John 1:12). At the foot of the cross the woman hears her new identity as "mother of the church" created, and there too, as at Cana, she says to us all, "Do whatever he tells you," knowing that like her we will be changed.

†

FOUR

The Father

"I have glorified, and I will glorify again." (John 12:28)

When God—the Father—speaks, the divine voice has a certain recognizable tone. At a few crucial points in the Gospels, we hear a divine voice that interprets and affirms the action and destiny of Jesus in a theophany, a revelation both of the Son and the Father. Of course, it may seem remarkable that God speaks at all, but it is the more striking that the divine voice seems to be distinguishable, even from just a few phrases across different texts.

In the baptism stories, a voice from heaven says "you are my son, the beloved; with you I am pleased" (Mark 1:11). Then at the Transfiguration, we can recognize the same voice, which speaks along the lines of "this is my son, the beloved; listen to him" (Mark 9:7). John's Gospel also depicts the scene of baptism and the descent of the dove, but there are no divine words heard. John also omits, and perhaps does

11 Conversations at the Cross

not need, a Transfiguration, because the mysterious power of Jesus is always bursting through the pages of the text in that Fourth Gospel. We can almost imagine the evangelist looking blankly at us for asking such a question as "when does the Father speak?," because for John what Jesus says is always what the Father says.

Yet there is in John one closer parallel to those stories, in a quite different scene, where just before the Last Supper and the Passion Narrative that unmistakable divine voice is heard. Jesus has just entered Jerusalem at the Passover, and is apparently still among the crowds. Some Greeks have asked to see Jesus, and this gives rise to a soliloquy for him where Jesus tells those who can hear him about his real identity. Yet in this one case, the soliloquy becomes a divine conversation. Jesus acknowledges, unusually, given the powerful presence he typically exudes, that his "soul is troubled," and he calls out:

> "What shall I say? 'Father, save me from this hour'? No, for this I have come, for this hour. Father, glorify your name." Then came a voice out of heaven: "I have glorified, and I will glorify again." (John 12:27–28)

Jesus continues, speaking to the startled bystanders who wonder if this has been an angel, or just thunder: "This voice has come for your sake, not for mine. Now is the judgment of this world, now shall the ruler of this world be cast out; and I, when I am lifted up from the earth, will draw all people to myself." (John 12:30b–32)

So there is a voice from heaven in John after all, and while it is not at the cross, it foreshadows quite directly that lifting up on the cross, a glorification greater even than the Transfiguration. Uniquely though, the voice in this case is more than a commentary to the onlooker or recorder, as in those baptism and Transfiguration stories. In those other cases, the divine voice had spoken in absolute terms, history itself the only real audience as God's utterance frames the scene with its awesome commentary. Here however, the Father speaks to the Son. This is actually the only conversation between the Father and the Son in the Gospels, between that human one whom we have come to understand is the presence and voice of God, now momentarily faltering in the mode of his concurrent true humanity as he faces the reality of his task with complete honesty and faith, and the transcendent God with whom he is one, and yet on whom he must rely at this rare moment of fragility.

Jesus had asked "what shall I say?" His dilemma turns out to be a choice, not just between statements, but between requests, or prayers. He at least considers, but sets aside, the understandable plea to ask for deliverance, "save me from this hour." This is not so far from the plea that Mark and Matthew record from the cross itself, "why have you abandoned me?" There the vulnerable Jesus's need to be delivered descended into what is often described as a cry of despair, but is actually a question too.

Here in John however, that possibility appears, and is resolved, before Jesus ever reaches the cross. Jesus instead answers the question himself and calls out to the Father, "Glorify your name!" And still, in this unique divine conversation, God does answer: "I have," it says; "I have glorified [it], and will glorify [it] again." Jesus's further response then explains just what this glorification means: "I, when I am lifted up from the earth, will draw all people to myself." So while the divine voice does not appear at the cross, we are to understand that the glory made known in this conversation will appear there.

This witness to glory is true even in that more desolate version of the question, "my God, my God," whereby Jesus on the cross addresses the Father. The need to ask it reveals the reality of what God has done in Christ, showing a glory that is not like the glory of the world. While power in human hands always means determining who can be controlled and manipulated, the power of God on the cross is the acceptance of human weakness and mortality, of God's being controlled by our indifference and cruelty. Even Jesus's word of dereliction, of abandonment, is itself a sign of that glory.

The answer to Jesus's question to the Father in Jerusalem, as well as the questions he asks on the cross, is "I have glorified, and will glorify again." And the familiarity of the divine voice allows us to understand that not only the voice, but the answer, is essentially the same one given at Jesus's baptism, and on the mount of the Transfiguration. The Father has glorified and will glorify the one who calls on him and speaks with him: "this is my son, the beloved; listen to him."

†

FIVE

Longinus

"Truly this Man was the Son of God." (Mark 15:39)

The picture of Roman brutality in the Passion Narrative is oppressive, but not simple. The Gospel pictures vary as to how much ambiguity or even sympathy for the soldiers they can allow to mitigate the picture of their words and actions, just as they vacillate towards the soldiers' master and Jesus' judge, the governor Pilate.

Matthew, Mark, and John all depict the scene of mockery by the soldiers during the trial, and the ironic cry "Hail, King of the Jews." Matthew and Mark also record that they offer Jesus drugged wine before he is crucified, possibly a sign of compassion, unless it is just to make the job easier. Then there is the famous dice game the soldiers played for his clothing, which does not reek of sympathy. The experienced gallows crew tries its proven anesthetic method again when the thirsting Jesus, calling out, is offered cheap wine on a spear. One soldier even shows some theological curiosity at this point, wondering whether Elijah might come and take him down. In John there also appears the story of Jesus's side being pierced with a spear, blood and water proceeding from this last expedient and violent act, undertaken just to make sure the team could go home on time.

These soldiers are the bad people of the gospel story, in the most concrete terms possible. Others betray, accuse, collude; these however are men not just of words but of action, who take hammers and spikes and spears and thorns, and do the whole bloody business while the others talk. And it only seems worse that those hints of normality, curiosity, sympathy, remind us that these are real people and not merely stock characters. People, people capable of seeing what is wrong with what they are doing, really do these things.

Poet Bruce Dawe imagines the more-in-sorrow-than-anger attitude of one of these hard-bitten Romans:

> Silenus
> held the spikes steady and I let fly
> with the sledge-hammer, not looking
> on the downswing trying hard not to hear
> over the women's wailing the bones give way
> the iron shocking the dumb wood.
>
> Orders is orders, I said after it was over
> nothing personal you understand—we had a
> drill-sergeant once thought he was God but he wasn't
> a patch on you...[1]

---

1. Bruce Dawe, *Sometimes Gladness: Collected Poems, 1954–1978* (Melbourne: Longman Cheshire, 1978), 192; and see Dennis Haskell, *Attuned to Alien Moonlight: The Poetry of Bruce Dawe* (Brisbane: University of Queensland Press, 2002), 223–24.

Longinus

As with the thieves, the shadowy picture of the soldiers at the cross has encouraged speculation about their real experiences, motives, and even identities. Dawe invents a "Silenus" for his version, which might well be told from the point of view of the (unnamed, in the poem) leader of the bunch, the centurion. This familiar tendency to elaborate the story has given the centurion a name in the tradition, Longinus.

The most remarkable moment for these Romans, and a remarkable one in the Gospel tradition as a whole, comes at the point of Jesus's death. It is not Mary, or John, or anyone who knew Jesus or who was among the good people, but our Longinus, the centurion in charge—the man who oversaw the whole bloody process—who becomes the first person in the whole Gospel story to name Jesus for who he really is: "Truly this man was the Son of God" (Mark 15:39).

It is tempting not just to elaborate but to moralize and psychologize these stories, where few clues are given as to what motivates the actors. We create fantasies about biblical characters whose inner lives are not revealed by narratives whose interests lie elsewhere, and so we make these players in our own image, or at least in images that suit our worldview. Cain must always have been a bad man, surely Abraham knew God didn't mean it about Isaac, and so on. Might Longinus then, this Roman soldier who is deemed worthy of gruesome responsibility by his masters, and who also confesses Jesus, have been the good guy? Was he responsible for the glimpses of empathy or pity amid the awful scene, and maybe even quite unhappy about the whole goings-on?

We have no real reason at all to think this. It would be more honest to assume that, like the rest of his crew, Longinus had become inured to the cruelty of his work; all we have seen of the whole team is all we can attribute to him. Perhaps this makes him a figure even more to be feared, or pitied; bitter, cynical, fully adequate to the tasks of oppression that depend on his compliance. "Thank you for your service," indeed.

This story isn't worth telling because Longinus was good, it's worth telling because Jesus is. Longinus, the man with oppression and injustice and cruelty baked on to him, speaks the truth about Jesus despite himself, and so do we. Longinus is an image of how people—truth be told, most people—have accommodated themselves to systems that require their cooperation, not just against virtue but against their own best interests. Sin isn't just a matter of the indifference of a few hard-bitten solders to banging in a few nails, it's the whole set of ideas and interests that had set this life in front of them to take.

One of the dubious hallmarks of contemporary society and politics, across its manifestly fractured state, is moralism. Across the divides of partisanship, mutual finger-pointing tends to devolve to the identification of "good people" and "bad people." The country and the world are in a mess, we all know, because of bad people, whether in leadership or in their retinues. And of course, it's true; what isn't true, or true enough, is our own sense of the good and the bad. More importantly, we should own up to God's lack of respect for these well-grounded distinctions or claims to truth, whatever they are. The moralizing division easily becomes a way of deflecting evil onto those whose lack of real power has given them certain roles, while ignoring our own place in the same systems.

The church is often at grave risk of joining in the game that judges and divides people in ways God does not. The

Gospels are full of stories about the wrong people being saved and the indignation that arises: the elder son's anger at the prodigal, the laborers' complaint about their wages, the dismay at the repentance of Zacchaeus, all of which cut across our tendencies to moralize where God will not. Perhaps we think that the temptation for the church is to stand with the respectable and powerful; this is, indeed, an abiding risk. But there is also the temptation to stand with the "good." Jesus does not do this. On the cross, Jesus is with everyone who has been the subject of deserved as well as undeserved scorn, with every wrongdoer as well as with every innocent sufferer. He will not allow either the perpetrator or the accuser to retreat to places of assurance and immobility, but will reach in and heal even what we do not especially want to be healed, in others and in ourselves.

In recording the unlikely witness of Longinus, Mark and the other evangelists are attesting not to his goodness, but to a remarkable reversal brought about at the cross. What Longinus says is therefore no easier a thing to hear than any of the other and more bruising words the soldiers speak, if we consider the source. Just as the label on the cross, the words of another Roman, state divine truth despite themselves, Longinus's conversation with Jesus tells us something true. It is not just that this man is the Son of God, but that he will speak with whom he chooses, and call whom he calls.

SIX

The Silence of the Angels

We have noted more than once how the story of Jesus's cross involves symmetry both with the story of creation as a whole, and with the story of his own creation, the incarnation. For all the scandal and struggle of the cross, we find there the fruitful completion of a work begun long before.

There is at least one significant missing piece among the parallels or threads to draw together at the cross, and accordingly we find one expected conversation decidedly lacking. Angels are always onstage in the divine drama, present to announce, to help, to warn, to sing the chorus behind the action that takes place as the human story plays out on the earthly stage. In the beginning, at creation itself, the angels play a part; Genesis itself does not mention them directly, but they are part of what comes into being; in the book of Job, the divine voice asks if Job were present when God "laid the foundations of the earth . . . when the morning stars sang together and all the heavenly beings (lit. 'Sons of God') shouted for joy" (Job

11 Conversations at the Cross

38: 4, 7). In the middle story, of incarnation, angels are also particularly prominent, and vocal. Angels appear and speak to both of Jesus's parents; most famously the angel Gabriel announces the birth of Jesus to Mary ahead of time, with his famous "Hail." A host of angels appears to the shepherds at the time of the birth, their presence and song announcing the identity of the one they are hymning, and his divine origin.

Angels however are absent at the crucifixion. In fact they are specifically and clearly absent, something underlined by mentions of them quite close to this moment, in the stories of Jesus's struggle with his fate on the Mount of Olives. Angels can accompany those who undergo trials and undertake journeys, as Raphael accompanies Tobias in the book of Tobit. This is as close as we get in the passion story when in the garden, according to Luke, Jesus falters, and there an angel strengthens him (Luke 22:53). This is the last angelic appearance though, at this final point of preparation for the journey to Golgotha, and the angel travels no further with him. Jesus must make this last journey alone.

Angels can fight in heavenly wars, as Michael prince of the angels does in the book of Daniel. Yet here at this greatest of battles, Jesus has no supporting forces. The way he explains this himself is telling. According to Matthew's story of the garden, at the very point where they come to seize Jesus, he says, "Do you think that I cannot appeal to my Father, and he will at once send me more than twelve legions of angels? But how then should the scriptures be fulfilled, that it must be so?" (Matt 26:53–4). Jesus must fight this last battle alone.

At the cross then, the angels are absent, or at least silent; for this work to be done, they must allow Jesus to meet his fate and not intervene. The story of the cross cannot be redeemed by the notion that Jesus is not really alone, or not facing the silence both of God and of the angels. Before, there were messages of comfort or strengthening, but at the cross there are no edifying, let alone glorious, sounds to mitigate the jeers and the weeping.

The meaning of the angelic silence however is not merely that these heavenly armies must stand by as the forces of evil triumph, true as that may be. The silence is their acknowledgment that the eternal Word of the Father, through whom all things were spoken into being at the beginning, is being silenced in death. Any other word would be hollow now, until his own last words are spoken and everything has been finished.

For the presence as well as the words of angels, we must now wait until after this silence is over. An angel of the Lord will come from heaven to roll away the stone that stopped up the mouth of the grave in the silence of death (Matt 28:2), and meet the women who come to the tomb and speak to them, as years before a woman had heard an angel speak, and tell them to go where that first angelic message had been given: "behold, he is going before you to Galilee; there you will see him." And as though to underline that the silence has now been broken, that angel will finish with an unusual phrase underlining this point: "See, I have told you" (Matt 28:7). Yes, an angel is speaking again.

Jesus had earlier spoken of another time when the angels would be present and not be silent: "For the Son of man is to come with his angels in the glory of his Father" (Matt 16:27) and "he will send out his angels with a loud trumpet call, and they will gather his elect from the four winds" (Matt 24:31). This further and future fanfare means a new creation, in which the struggling and suffering world finds itself remade, along with the dead Jesus. The silence of oppression and degradation at the cross will give way to the trumpet sound, when all the heavenly beings again shout for joy as at the beginning, and angels again have their say.

SEVEN

Nicodemus

"How can someone be born when they are old?" (John 3:4)

The last person who is named in the narrative of John about the crucifixion of Jesus is Nicodemus, who long before "had at first come to him by night" (John 19:39; cf. 3:2). When Joseph of Arimathea takes the dead body of Jesus, which all the Gospels report, John also tells us this same Nicodemus came, "bringing a mixture of myrrh and aloes, about a hundred pounds' weight."

These two men are unique among those identified as Jesus's followers in the Gospels, in that they are both powerful and respectable people, identified as a member of the Sanhedrin and a "ruler" of the Jews respectively. No one else makes these two lists of the privileged and the disciples. Many people follow Jesus of course, but most are unremarkable. There are a few other wealthy ones like Zacchaeus, but he was a despised tax collector. There are other powerful people in the narrative, but they are not followers. So these two are unusual, and have a lot to lose. Although they are among the most privileged of the characters in the story, now their greatest privilege, something that others could not or would not be able to exercise, is to receive and to lay to rest the body of Jesus.

When Jesus had met Nicodemus earlier, Nicodemus came secretly, and their encounter gave rise to a famous conversation about the need for rebirth. Nicodemus opened that exchange in fairly flat-footed terms, affirming that Jesus must have been sent from God because of the signs he does. It seems Nicodemus is an empiricist, taking in what he sees and knows, while apparently not wanting to be seen and known so much himself. Jesus responds—obliquely, it seems at first—that unless someone is born anew (or from above) they cannot see the kingdom of God. Nicodemus plays his part in the familiar tendency for Jesus's interlocutors in this Gospel to misunderstand, and acts as foil for him: "How can someone be born when they have become old?" (John 3:4). By implication, Nicodemus is an old man himself.

Jesus's explanatory response, which seems like a massive change of subject, has become a point of historic misunderstanding or contention for Christians ever since; for the same Greek word means both "anew" and "from above," so that Jesus may indeed be saying to Nicodemus "you must be born a second time," or just "born again," but also, in the very same word, "you must be born from above," from some different, higher, realm. Some strands of Christianity have held this passage hostage to certain forms of religious experience, of being "born again" as a narrowly defined sort of conversion moment. Yes, we must all be born again; but while some people have experiences that start their new life in a moment, far more will find their new beginnings are harder, and longer, like actual births.

The second possible meaning, of birth "from above," is at least equally present in the conversation, given that Jesus goes on to say to Nicodemus "unless one is born of water and the Spirit, they cannot enter the kingdom of God." All this still begs the question of what second or different birth, what new kind of being, what new and different life from above. Yes, you must be born again, from above; but how?

The real meaning of that other birth seems to be revealed in this story of the cross. This is a complete transformation of the self, as dramatic as natural birth and more dangerous. Jesus had told Nicodemus that "as Moses lifted up the serpent in the wilderness, so must the son of man must be lifted up so that whoever believes in him may have eternal life" (John 3:14–15). This is clearer now; new life may only come, it seems, through death, and through this one death in particular.

The Nicodemus who comes with Joseph to the tomb has changed since we first encountered him. He did appear once more in the meantime, when there was a dispute about Jesus and an early attempt to arrest him. Nicodemus then objected to his fellows among the Jewish leaders at a possible rush to judgment about Jesus, in terms that confirmed his concern for the evidence: "Does our law," he says, "judge a man without first giving him a hearing and learning what he does?" (John 7:51). When Nicodemus appears again here at the end of the story, though, he has apparently given Jesus the hearing that he deserves, and passed his own judgment. He is no longer Jesus's follower only by night. The old man now comes to the cross in the daylight, unmistakable and convinced, transformed even, in a public act of compassion and allegiance, taking the body that has been exposed and tested, and not ashamed to be seen offering this last act of care.

But Nicodemus's return at this point tells us about more than just his own transformation. His reappearance is our clue that their dialogue is continuing, even at the grave, a prelude to something yet to be spoken that will reveal the true meaning of the conversation long before. Nicodemus's and Joseph's actions constitute the end of Jesus's body as it had been known, born once of Mary. When, early on the first day, a different Mary comes to seek it, the stone will be rolled away, and Jesus will now truly have been born again, and from above. The body with which he appears, the unmistakable sign that Jesus indeed comes from God as Nicodemus had dared hope before, is both like and unlike the body that Mary bore, and which Joseph and Nicodemus carried to the grave. Still bearing the imprints of the nails, but also bearing the glory of his new creation, this body is the first fruits of new birth to the exalted life that Jesus has promised Nicodemus, and us.

This, then, is how someone can be born when they are old. To follow Jesus is to be born again, and from above, the beginning of a life more fully transformed than any of our religious allegiances and experiences can themselves possibly effect in isolation. Not our decisions or actions, but God's call that once brought Jesus to new birth, will do this for us, as it did once for old Nicodemus.

www.ingramcontent.com/pod-product-compliance
Lightning Source LLC
Chambersburg PA
CBHW051133160426
43195CB00014B/2458